HOW TO EARN MONEY ONLINE WITHOUT INVESTMENT

31 effective ways to earn a good income from home + BONUS

By

K. A. Patil

Table of Contents

Introduction

Today most of the people have smart phones in their hands, whole day... Smart phones and computer/laptops have become so much important in our lives that we can't even imagine our lives without them...

But you all are going to agree on this fact that spending most of the time on internet is not giving you any money in return... This is one of the biggest disadvantages that people see with the increase in use of internet worldwide... According to people those who are spending their most of the time on internet are actually wasting their time instead of going something solid to earn good income...

No one wants to work under anybody but we are forced into it, as we don't find any solid way to earn money and run our houses from any other way... I have been struggling with the same problem but it was my passion to earn money from home without investment and finally I am a successful online earner...

I have been working online for the last 6 years... If I would say it literally then I was not only working online but also trying to find out all the ways through which you can earn a good monthly income from home... This book is the result of that research... I didn't have money to investment in anything and start working to earn in return. So, I only concentrated on the ways to 'earn money from home without any investment'. Here I found 31 ultimate ways to earn a good income online without actually investing anything...

It is more of a guide about those ways as if I would have at least tried to explain each on them in detail. Then one book for each would not have been good enough to explain them fully. I have seen people struggling to find genuine ways to earn money from home with no money in hand. But internet is a wide world with lots and lots of things that can mislead us...

It is quite hard to find something genuine as well as useful, that too in a short period of time... You can see it actually took me 6 years to only find 31 real effective ways... so to cut short your work load as well as start working as soon as possible on internet to earn. I finally decided to share all the ways that I found through my online research...

You can get a very good idea about all the ways mentioned in this book and then grab more knowledge according to your interested field...

Earning money online and running your home effectively with that money is hard to do but still it is not that impossible....as you think..

So, explore all the ways of this book and find your passionate one to start... Work from your homes and spend the rest of the time with your families to show your love to them... You can also implement only 2-3 hours daily in any of these mentioned ways and see enough money coming into your bank a/c on regular basis... To make the income regular you have to invest at least some time daily...

Get paid up to 300$ to write

If you are trying to earn a good income from internet then it is one of the most important qualities to know how to write about anything. Writing is the basic step to start earning a good income online. But you don't worry if you are not at all good at writing or have never ever written a single paragraph by yourself then too you can earn a real good income from online.

As I know that it was I who mentioned writing as an important quality to earn money from internet. But still it is not the only quality that will help you in earning online…. So, apart from this if you are really good at writing then you should definitely take an advantage from this step to start earning a very good income sitting at your very homes….

There are a lot of websites present through web that allows you to write for them and earn a good income from your writing…. Some provide you topics, some tell you to choose topics on your own, some has word limits, some has not… every site carries its own T & C to write for them. But one thing that is common in all of the below ones is that they are going to pay you for your work once approved… This is the only important thing that really matters…

According to my research all the sites listed below can pay you as much as 300 $ per article or essay or post you write. The general procedure for this is you have to visit the site first to be aware about the latest information on writing and submitting your work… Also you will get an exact idea about how much you are going to get paid per writing sample…

You might be thinking that I should have given a little description of all these sites. You are absolutely right… I also thought to do so but I noticed that these sites change their terms of writing every now and then. So, if I mentioned anything in the information section of all of them and then if they updated it.

Then you all will think that I tried to mislead all of you to grab more and more attention. So, ultimately I decided that it will be better if I give an overview about all these and provide you with the real names or address of the websites to find out as much as you want to know…..to start working….

I have made a combined list of websites that accepts essays, articles, or posts and pay you according to your work, word limit and uniqueness of the writing sample…. Once these sites approve your work then they will pay you according to it…. Here are 20 sites that will pay you up to 300 $ per sample you write for them…

1. Essig magazine
2. https://hubpages.com/signin/
3. Vox – first person
4. Lighthouse-sf.org
5. Nytimes.com
6. Skirt.com
7. The establishment
8. Narrative.ly
9. Aish.com
10. http://alistapart.com/
11. Alaskaparent.com/
12. Theexpenditiones.com
13. Internationalliving.com
14. Wisebread.com
15. Maketecheasier.com
16. Techopedia.com
17. Photoshoptutorials.ws
18. http://www.toptenz.net/
19. http://listverse.com/
20. Eurekastreet.com.au
21. Peopleperhour.com
22. https://afineparent.com/write
23. https://ecommerceinsiders.com/write/
24. The Penny Hoarder
25. https://www.smashingmagazine.com/write-for-us/
26. https://www.photoshoptutorials.ws/money-photoshop/
27. https://alistapart.com/about/contribute/
28. https://code.tutsplus.com/articles/call-for-authors-write-for-tuts--cms-22034
29. https://greatescapepublishing.com/program/travel-writing/
30. https://writenaked.net/guest-blog-writers/
31. https://www.sitepoint.com/get-paid-write-html-css-sass/

32. https://internationalliving.com/about-il/write-for-il/write-for-international-living-magazine/
33. https://design.tutsplus.com/articles/call-for-authors-get-paid-for-writing-for-vectortuts--vector-14108
34. https://www.uxbooth.com/contribute/
35. https://www.digitalocean.com/community/pages/write-for-digitalocean
36. https://code.tutsplus.com/articles/interested-in-writing-for-wptuts-read-on--wp-34446
37. https://www.cracked.com/article_19955_we-want-to-pay-you-to-write-us.html

Indian Writers (beginners)

If you are an Indian and want to start a career in writing then you should start with some easy sites…. The below listed names allow you to set up a career in the field of writing and start earning as soon as possible… These sites are not going to pay you a very big amount per article you write for them but still they will pay you good to write as a beginner…..

The basic difference between the above mentioned 20 sites and these 4 is that they may not prove to be a regular or daily source of income for you… but the below sites will give you as much as work you want to do… If you concentrate on your work as much as possible then you will increase your earnings in no time….

1. http://iwriter.com/
2. http://constentcontent.com/
3. ayushveda.com/
4. http://expertcolumn.com

Well, the following list specializes for short story writing. Check them out too.

- https://agnionline.bu.edu/submit
- https://www.analogsf.com/contact-us/writers-guidelines/
- https://thesunmagazine.org/submit
- https://www.one-story.com/?page=submit
- https://dailysciencefiction.com/submit
- https://www.carvezine.com/submit
- https://penpee.com/how-it-works/

ONLINE RESELLING – sell anything online

Online reselling is the newest and most trendy business idea nowadays. Coming straight to the point what online reselling is, it means re-selling anything online. Now the question appears that what is reselling? Reselling is selling something that is sold by somebody else or simply selling others' products.

I know you might be thinking right now that if you will sell others' products then how you can earn money or make any profit. When you work as a Reseller for any seller, the sellers will send you product details with images daily on your whatsapp, you just have to add your profit with their price and share them in your social networks and grab orders. When you get the order you have to collect the payment from the customer and pay the amount to the seller (excluding your profit) and confirm the order. Then, you have to send the address of the customer with his contact number and below you have to mention your name and number, to the seller.

I will teach you how to be an expert in this field and earn 30k – 50k per month. If you follow the step by step procedure, you can definitely achieve that goal or even more. These are the steps to do online reselling.

- Create social media accounts
- Find genuine wholesalers
- Crosscheck them before you start working for them
- Use social media accounts to get orders
- Payment procedure
- Expand your contacts
- Hire resellers – Make people work for you

Create social media accounts – Social media accounts are really very important to do online reselling. Most of us have at least one FB account so it is a plus point. You can use your own FB account or you can create a new one. The benefit of your own FB account is that it will help people know about your startup but if you want to do this business privately then you can create a new account too.

Just the extra benefit of your own FB account is that the people who already trust you will give you orders if they know about your startup and your personal FB account will do that for you. Now, you need to install and use some other chatting apps such as whatsapp, hike, viber etc …… and as much as you want.

Create an account in Google+, as it is also a very good place to get orders. For beginners you must have a Face book (FB), Whatsapp and Google+ account. Install all these 3 apps in your phone to work conveniently.

Find genuine wholesalers – You are going to sell others products so it is definite that you need somebody who let you sell their products adding your profits in their prices. As you can see that I have mentioned sellers in the above example but telling you to find genuine "wholesalers". Why wholesaler? Because if you work for a seller, he will send you the price after adding his own profit in the price and there will be less room for your profit. You didn't know the actual price of the product and how much profit he had added.

There is a huge chance that after adding your profit the product become totally expensive and that also increases the fear that your customer can get that product at lower price from somebody else. For example – If the actual price of the product is 300 (wholesale price) and the seller have send you 500 (after adding his profit) now, you also added 100 in that price and forwarded it to the customers. You can see that after all this process the price got doubled from 300 to 600.

When somebody comes to know that you are selling something in 600 whose actual price is 300 then it spoils your name as well as trust in front of the customers. But, think that if you got that product direct from the wholesalers then you can easily sell it and make extra profit too.

So, the bottom line is that, if you sell products direct from the wholesalers you can add more profit to the product and eventually earn more.

Crosscheck them before start working for them – Even if they are wholesalers still you have not seen them, visited their shops or factories or may be even their city. It is really important to crosscheck them because you are going to pay them first and then they are going to deliver the product to your customers.

If after paying the amount the wholesaler didn't deliver the product then everything will come up to you and you have to bare the loss, so to protect that, you just have to crosscheck the wholesalers and make sure that he/she is genuine and you can trust them with the valuable money of your customers.

Use social media for reselling - This is the main work that you have to do as a reseller. The product details that you will get daily from your wholesalers you have to share them with your social networking accounts. It is very simple "the more you share, the more order you will get". As sharing will let people know about the products you have.

Payment Procedure – When you get orders then your main responsibilities start from here. First you have to collect the payment from the customer and pay it to confirm the order as soon as the product goes out of stock. After the dispatch of the order the wholesalers will give you the picture of dispatch slip. You have to forward it to the customer, as your customer can track their order through this slip.

Expand contacts – As the name indicates that you have to grow your circle and increase your contacts to get more and more orders. Some of you would already have a good amount of friends and contacts but if you don't, then my tested ways can help you build your contacts and develop your startup business.

Hire resellers – It is the most necessary step to earn a good monthly income from online reselling. From the above steps you will learn reselling completely and will start earning also but to earn an amount that can run your house, you have to follow this step.

When I started reselling through my FB account, at first my friends asked about the products that I post on my wall but when they came to know that I was doing it from home and earning a good income then eventually they started to take interest in this work.

Every now and then I started getting messages from my friends asking about online reselling, how you do it, what is the procedure, can we earn really, can I do it, when can I start etc...etc... I explained the whole procedure to a lot of people some of them started working for me and some used my ways to do it.

I will explain how you can earn more if more and more people start working as resellers for you. See you are working for wholesalers, sharing their products to your contacts, social accounts etc… and getting orders for them.

They don't have to spend money in marketing of their products, don't have to hire sales persons, no need to find customers and explain them anything or convince them to buy, or apply any efforts to get orders, as all this is done by you and they just have to be in their places and deliver the product to the customers made by you.

Now just imagine if people start working as resellers for you then you just have to send regular updates to your resellers, which you get from your wholesalers and they will do all the hard work for you to bring more and more orders, as they want to earn too. More order means more money and more active reseller means more orders. The resellers that are very active in their work and use all their contacts and efforts to get orders and earn a good income are known as active resellers. You need people work for you as resellers but you will get extra benefits in your earning with active resellers only.

Active resellers are more beneficial than just resellers so, just encourage your resellers to be active and get more orders. But, overall hiring more resellers will help you grow your monthly income. It is obvious that when you start earning as reseller, people will ask you about what you do and will show interest in this work.

You just have to explain all this procedure and recommend them to join you or you can say that if they want, you will send your regular updates of the products and they can start reselling.

TIP – When you explain anybody about the procedure of reselling don't share that wholesalers' part. As if everybody will know about the difference between sellers and wholesalers then who will buy from you or work for you. You just mention that you get the products direct from some trusted wholesalers and you worked so hard to find them and work with them.

This is an overview of "Online Reselling" but after reading this if you think that you should get full knowledge on this topic then you can have a look on my book "Online Reselling – A Startup Without Investment" By K. A. Patil. It's a complete step by step guide to do online reselling in a perfect way to earn more and more money from home.

You can visit my author page to get all my books – https://www.amazon.com/author/kapatil

BLOGGING

You might have heard about his one as it is one of the most popular as well as oldest online earning ways. If you do it in the right way then it can be a great source of long term income. First of all you have to set up a blog you can do it for free through Blogger or Word Press. I have used Blogger for a very long period of time. So I can give you some tips to earn a good income through blogging on Blogger. You just have to sign up on Blogger using your Google account and then set- up your blog.

Before you sign up on Blogger take some time to decide the title of your blog as well as the topic or genre you want to write posts on. It will a lot more beneficial for you if you create a specific topic or category based blog. As specific niche based blog are easy to make them searchable on search engines.

For example – If you love to talk about relationships then you can create a blog on this category, if you are a health expert or a fitness freak then you can create a blog related to this niche, if you can cook variety of dishes in a different way or you know a lot of recipes or you are interesting in topics like cooking, baking etc… then you can choose this one.

Any topic on which you think that you will be comfortable in writing posts then you can decide the name and address of your blog according to that. Just remember that the name of your blog should represent the category of your blog or the topic on which it is based.

Like – If you love to cook and have some old family secrets for quick and easy cooking. So share the knowledge through blog. Suppose a food blog based on vegetarian recipes can be named as "Veg Food Love" http://vegfoodlove.blogspot.in/

See this blog name will easily give an idea to the readers that it's about vegetarian cooking. So it is quite important that your blog name should represent the idea behind its creation.

SEO friendly posts

Before you start looking for some ways through which you can earn money from your blog. First you should make at least 5 – 10 SEO friendly posts on your blog. By the SEO friendly post I mean that you should make post with suitable keywords at right places. You should not do keyword stuffing in your post. When you make a blog post make sure that you have all these.

- Decide a title as well as subtitle.
- Make a list of key words you want to use in your post.
- You can use any free or paid keyword search for this. I haven't used it yet but if you want then you sure can.
- Use those keywords in the title.
- Now write a blog post using some of these keywords here and there but don't overdo it.
- Highlight these keywords with bold or italics, as it will make it easy for search engines to find.
- Write a post with at least 500 or more words, as Google loves more data.
- Most important point is just trying to be simple as well as original in your content.
- Keep these points in mind and write minimum 5 – 10 posts on your blog.

Search engine settings

- Sign in to your blogger account.
- Go to setting -> search preference -> Meta tags.
- Write a suitable description about your blog with exact suitable keywords.
- Now go to crawlers and indexing -> custom robot header tags -> enable it.
- In it, home page -> tick 'all' and 'noodp'.
- Then archive and search pages -> tick 'noindex' and 'noodp'.
- Then default for posts and pages -> tick 'all' and 'noodp'.

Through these settings, you will be able to write a search description for your blog post (you can see 'search description column' visible in blog post writing area after applying above settings). Now add suitable labels to your posts and also add a quick catchable description.

You can also customize your post link to make it more suitable for search engines to make it visible during a search. You can do this through 'permalink' present on the right side while writing a post. Click on 'permalink' you will see two options

- Automatic
- Customize or custom

Click on customize to create your own post link. For example, once I wrote a post on earn money from home without investment and this was its link - http://justbefriendofyourself.blogspot.in/2017/05/earn-money-from-home-without-investment.html look at this 'blog post link' it easily shows that this post is about earn money from home without investment.

Suppose you have written a post about '10 ways to do SEO on a blog post', now you can add this in your link like 10-ways-to-do-SEO-on-a-blog-post. Just click on customize and write your desired suitable phrase by using the same method. Use hyphen or underscore between the words.

Changing your post link using this method in not that necessary if the automatic link created by it has nothing that can confuse anybody... You need to apply this step if your title of the post is too big as well as you have a subtitle. As because of all these there is possibility that your automatic link will contain some difficult coding or numbers in the link.

Any of these will not help in giving any idea about the title or topic on which the post is written... So, to avoid it you have to customize your link according to your blog title or anything you want to indicate.

These are the basic settings you can do to your blog to make it easy for the search engines to find your blog.

Site-map submission

Now you have created nearly 5 – 10 posts on your blog. It's time to make Google aware that you have created a good blog by submitting the site map of your blog on Google console. When you submit the sitemap of your blog on Google then it will be able to keep a track of your blog and its audiences.

- Go to settings -> then search preferences -> under crawlers and indexing.

- Go to Google search console -> click on edit.
- You will directed to a Google console (Google webmaster tools) page
- Click on 'add a property' button (red color).
- Enter your blog address and then click on 'add'.
- It will direct you to the verification page.
- There will be 2 verification ways present first 'recommended' one and other is 'alternate method'.
- Select alternate method -> then select 'HTML tag'.
- You will get a Meta tag for your home page. I know if you are not a technical person then it is a very difficult word for you understand. But don't worry you just follow these steps and you can achieve what you want.
- If you have not done this before then you can click on 'show me an example' to see where you have to put this given link.
- Just copy this link and go back to your blog.
- Don't close this page as after putting this link on your home page you have to come back to verify it.
- Now on your blog go to theme -> then you can an option 'edit html'.
- Click on it.
- As you have seen in the example you have to put this verification link just below the 'head'.
- If you are unable to find the head section then you can search it using ctrl+f.
- Enter this link just below the <head>.
- After this click on 'save theme' to save it.
- Now go back to Google console page and click on 'verify' to complete the verification process.
- Your site is verified now.
- Go to home -> and click on your blog name.
- You will be directed to your Google console dashboard.
- Click on sitemap.
- Click on 'add/test sitemap'.
- You might be thinking that you don't have to a sitemap then how you will submit it.
- Don't worry just visit http://ctrlq.org/blogger/

- Enter your full blog address in the given space.
- Now click on 'generate sitemap'.
- You will get you sitemap to submit it on Google.
- Just copy it and submit it.

You have successfully submitted your sitemap to Google. Now Google will be able to keep an eye on your posts.

These are some ways to do blogging in a proper way...

Now it's time to set up ways to start earning from your blog. There are a lot of ways available online to earn money from your blog. Some of them are as follows-

Google Ad sense

It is the most popular way to earn money through blogger. You might have heard about it surely but if not then I will give you a general overview of it. Google Ad sense will give you some ads to show it on your blog and blog posts. If someone clicks on any of these ads then Google Ad sense will pay you for that click.

It is the most popular way and better from affiliate program, because it is paying you for each and every click. Unlike affiliate programs you don't have to sell anything to earn commission.

It somewhat makes sure that if you get approved from Google Ad sense then you will definitely earn a good monthly income. Google Ad sense will offer you ads related to your blog niche or ads relating to your blog post which increases the chances that if someone visits your blog post then they will surely click on the ads related to your blog post.

And you will be surely getting paid for those clicks. So, it is important as well as beneficial for you to get an approval from it. I will tell you the basic procedure to do it and get approval.

Once you have made some good posts on your blog and got some good views then you will be able to see the sign up option for Google Ad sense in the earnings tab of your blogger dashboard. Just click on it and fill the required details to submit your proposal.

After your submission, it will take some time or even days to give the result. You will be informed through mail that your application is approved or not. If you don't get approval then don't worry you can reapply after a few more posts or after you have increased your overall blog views.

Also I will advise you to make some pages for your blog before you apply for Ad sense. Go to the pages section of your bloggers dashboard and make pages like 'About me'. It is the most important one that Google Ad sense searches for to give approval.

You can simply introduce yourself in this page. You can also create a 'contact me' page and share your social media details to get more connected with your readers.

I know that it is quite important to get approved through Ad sense but if you did not get an approval from it then it is not the end of the world. There are a lot of alternatives available to it such as

- media.net,
- ShareASale,
- LinkShare etc…

You can visit any of these and apply for approval to start earning through clicks.

Don't worry if you are not getting approval from these sites, there are a lot more ways available to earn from your blog.

Back-links

You must have heard about this topic whenever you search any knowledge on web to find ways for promoting your blog… I will make it really clear for you that what a back-link is… and why it is so much important for us to earn a good income from our blog or website… A back-link is the particular link of your blog post which we leave on other sites to increase our own audience from the traffic that comes on their websites…

Now you might be thinking that why other bloggers will allow you to put your link in their website and steal their traffic… But it is not like that… the sites that allow you to leave your back- links are designed according to that…

When you visit any blog you can see the comments section below it… Some sites allow you to leave your back-links and publish them… Now when somebody else clicks on that link, he will be directed to that particular post of your blog…. Some very basic and important points that you need to keep in mind while putting back-links are as follows-

You must post your back-links in sites that allows do-follow back-links. There are 2 types of back-links.

1. No-follow back-links
2. Do-follow back-links

No-follow back-links as the name indicates, whether you have put your back-links on a 100 websites but if they are no-follow back-links then it is kind of useless for us or our blog promotion…As the main purpose of back-linking is to get more and more traffic to our site.

If those links can't fulfill this purpose then they are of no use. Every site does not allow putting your link in its comments… If you still leave you back-link over there then your link will also behave like a plain text and nothing will be directed even on clicking on it a hundred times.

Do-follow back-links, you must have got an idea about this one. As it is just opposite to the above one…When somebody clicks on a do-follow back-link then it is directed to the page you want him to visit… There are a lot of awesome sites with amazing daily traffic that allows you to leave your do-follow back-links, and try to get some benefit from their traffic…

So, to increase your blog traffic with the help of back-links, you first need to search down some good traffic blogs or websites that allows you to leave do-follow back-links… Blogger allows you to leave do-follow back-links…and the best sites that I know to get the list of sites that allow leaving do-follow back-links is 'Shoutoutloud.com'.

You will get a regular knowledge about blogging, affiliate marketing and many more…. I was really wondering why I didn't get this site a little earlier, if I would have gotten this site earlier then I would have completed my research a lot sooner….

The next best way is -

Affiliate Marketing

As I mentioned it above that you will earn a commission per sale made by your posted links. You might be thinking that it is next to impossible to earn any money and earning money through Ad sense method was easier. You are half right and half wrong.

As you are right that earning through Ad sense was easier but it is not impossible to earn through Affiliate marketing, if you do it the right way. I will tell you the step by step procedure to do it and earn a good income regularly. First of all you have to apply for some affiliate programs if you are new then you should start with these 2.

Amazon Affiliate

I am an Indian and as per my experience it is best one for affiliate marketing. It has some features which other affiliate sites don't have. If we talk about Amazon India then its best feature is 'Site stripe', which allows you to get any page or product link direct from the Amazon shopping website.

You don't need to sign in to your affiliate dashboard to generate product links. But Amazon US has more features than Amazon India and its best one is 'native ads'.

- First of all visit Amazon and scroll down to see the option 'be an affiliate' or anything related to affiliate.
- Click on it to visit the affiliate site.
- Now click on sign up button to apply.
- Fill in the proper details and submit.
- Once you got your approval mail then login to complete your payments details.
- After all these you are now ready to starting posting products links.
- You can search for products on your affiliate home page but if you want then can simply login to Amazon shopping site and get links generated from there.
- Once you login to your Amazon account, search for anything.

- You will see an option on the top of the page like 'associate site stripe' or 'get the link'.
- You will see 3 options 'text' 'image' 'text + image'.
- You can easily understand that what type of ads these options can show like if you create a link by clicking 'text' then it will show only text in the ad and similarly 'image' will show images only and 'text + image' will show both.
- Click on any of it to generate your link of that product or page.
- Copy it and then paste it on your blog post.
- When you create a post then you can see an option of html near compose click on html and paste your product link.
- You can also add your affiliate links in between your posts by inserting links option.
- You can click on link option while creating a blog post, then paste your product link in between of your post.
- For example – If you have posted a review about a mobile phone on this blog post then you can insert the links of that phone from Amazon. You can also insert mobile related things in between the posts to get more and more from it.
- You can also share those links directly to face book and twitter from Amazon website.
- You can also make a FB page and then post these links to get more and more earnings from it as soon as possible. For example – I have created a page to post my Amazon affiliate links named 'Amazon Lovers' https://www.facebook.com/Onlineshoppinglovers/ you can visit it to see the posts. You will get an idea that how you can post your affiliate links to get more audiences. I haven't used the FB paid ads service to promote my posts but still I get good response from my posts.
- Join shopping related groups on FB and then share your page posts on these groups to get more customers.
- You can also save pictures from any Amazon page and copy the link of that page. Now create a post on your page with all those images with a short description with that copied page link.
- In this way you will be able to post a bunch of pictures and direct your customers directly to that page so that they can see a lot of options to buy.

- This increases the chances of getting a sale from your posted links.

Click Bank Affiliate

It is also one of the most popular affiliate programs to join. You just have to sign up for it with your blog details and once you got an approval mail then you can start posting product links to get a sale.

- Once you got approved login to your dashboard.
- On the upper side you can see an option 'marketplace' click on it.
- Here you can search for various products and generate links.
- Once you find a product that you want to promote then click on 'promote' to prepare link.
- A popup window will open click on create to generate link.
- Copy the link to and paste it on your blog post to make it visible for visitors after publishing that post.
- You can also share this link through your FB page.

To get an idea of click bank links you can see my FB page 'Funny Offers' https://www.facebook.com/funnyoffers/ to get full knowledge of it. I have created this page specially for posting my Click Bank product links.

There are a lot more things that are related to do successful affiliate marketing and if I will mention all those then I would have to write a full book on it. If you think that Click Bank will be a little tough for you then you can totally concentrate on Amazon.

As it is one of the most trusted shopping sites so will not need to convince the customers about its products you just have to post attractive products and make them reachable to right people. As I mentioned before about my book related to "Online Reselling", through that book you can also learn to make proper FB posts to get more and more customers.

One more amazing way to promote your affiliate links.

You can create a blog on *Tumblr*, oh it's a very effective way to market your affiliate links. It's a fast growing social media Platform. You can easily create an account on it. Additionally, on Tumblr, the biggest plus point is you can post almost 250 posts per day not limited to 2 – 3 posts per day unlike Facebook, Twitter or Instagram. Also, Tumblr allows you to post a link directly, as they have a post category for 'links' only. How cool is that, right!!!!

For Amazon affiliate links follow these steps –

- Go to Amazon website.
- As explained before, you will be able to see that 'Amazon Associates Site stripe'. Now from here, click on "text".
- Copy the link.
- Now go to your Tumblr blog to post it. Click on 'link'.
- Then paste this copied link in the 'type or paste a URL' section.
- Wait for a few seconds and you will be able to see the name and description of the product you have chosen to share.
- Now, below the details, you will be able to see add description. There on the right hand side, you can see few options for images, video, gif etc... Here we can add the images of that product.
- For images, come back on the Amazon product page and click on the product image and save it on your computer. (Left click > save image as).
- Once the images are saved, add them to your Tumblr blog post.
- Then add 'tags' (hastags) to your post and post it.

You can also share this Amazon 'text' links directly on your Whatsapp groups, Snapchat and any other chatting sites.

You might be thinking why this hassle of manually saving the images and then adding them to the post, when we also have 'text + image' link, right? You got a point but those 'image' and 'text + image' links are for posting ads on your blog. They are html links specially created according to html settings of a blog. As Tumblr allows us to share the link directly without any html settings, hence the 'image' or 'text + image' link will not work on Tumblr.

You can check this blog on Tumblr. It is created to share Amazon Affiliate links - https://bestdeals88.tumblr.com/

Get paid to write guest posts

In the starting I have given you a list of some sites that allows you to write for them and earn a good income from it... But here are some sites that allow you to write guest post for their sites and they will pay you for your post if they get approved... The one extra benefit of this guest posting is that you can include your do-follow back-links it your guest post and use this method to increase your own blog's traffic as well.

As per my word of wise you should write a guest post related to your own blog post. Mention some of the important points of your real post in your guest post and then leave your blog post link in the end to get them directed to that particular post of your blog…to read it fully… In this way you can market your own blog and even get paid for it…

Below is a list of 10 sites which are quite popular in the field of guest posting…

1. http://writenaked.net/
2. fundsforwriters.com/
3. cracked.com/
4. makealivingwriting.com/
5. thewritelife.com/
6. beafreelanceblogger.com/
7. http://knowledgenuts.com/
8. toplenz.net/
9. http://blog.iwawine.com/
10. http://www.bootsnall.com/

Get paid to write your own Blog Posts

Earn hundreds, even thousands, per month!

SponsoredReviews are looking for people who are passionate, honest and entertaining to write informative reviews of advertisers' products, services and websites – and post them on our blogs!

Use your own writing style to write positive reviews or to provide constructive criticism. (However, any rude, hateful or potentially libelous reviews will be declined by them.)

The advertisers present on this site are looking for honest opinions from real people like you – and they're willing to pay to get them!

You can earn as much as you'd like to write!

Currently, a number of bloggers are making a lot of extra cash every month by posting honest reviews for SponsoredReviews.com!

They have a huge marketplace of advertisers looking for bloggers. Every type of website you can possibly imagine needs a good exposure. And they're looking for good writers who are willing to talk about it, review it and spread the word about it!

You literally have dozens of opportunities in every category! From cultural websites to technical gadgets to general interest sites, no matter what you like to write about, you can now make a lot of money doing it!

And get this: You can also choose the advertisers you want to write for!

Here you can actually afford to be picky!

With so many websites and subjects to choose from, you'll be provided with a huge list of customers looking for some nice exposure via blog reviews like yours. Do the research; check out their sites, and then blog about the ones that excite you the most! Then bid on any project you like to write about.

Remember – 'The more you write, the more popular your blog will become!'

As you know, the first rule of blogging is "Post Often." If you blog every day or two, then people start to notice you. Your subscription rate goes up. And that drives high-quality search engine traffic to your site!

Their advertisers can come to your blog two ways:

1. List your blog in our marketplace of available reviewers! The advertisers will check your interests and the subjects covered by your blog, and they'll literally come to you! Then, you have the option to accept or decline any review request.
2. Search for advertisers directly! Their unique bidding system allows you to bid on jobs and negotiate your rates with advertisers. It's a great way to maximize your earnings!

Here's all you need to know to get started:

1. Register your blog(s) with SponsoredReviews.com.
2. Each blog needs to be at least three months old, with at least ten posts of real content.
3. Each blog you register needs to have unique, unshared content, and the reviews you post must be of your own creation, not copied from any other blog.
4. All reviews must appear on your blog homepage the day you submit it to them, and remain there for at least 24 hours.
5. Your blog must be indexed on all of the major search engines, including Google.

They Pay every 2 weeks via PayPal!

You can visit the website to see the tips and tricks to do blogging. It is explained you in detail that how you should write your blog posts, design the blog, and earn more and more money from this way... The above mentioned information is what they actually offer to the blogger and advises you to follow....

Some more ways to earn money through internet are-

Pay per clicks

These sites pay you for clicks and you don't need any blog or website to sign up for these sites. The one that I know is "Adfly" https://join-adf.ly/16871923 (you can use this link to sign up easily) you can just sign in using your FB account and follow these steps.

- Select any site.
- Copy its URL.
- Paste it on 'adfly' dashboard to shorten.
- Now you will get the link to share for getting clicks to get paid.
- Share that link through your social networking accounts like FB, G+, whatsapp etc... And as many as you want.
- When someone clicks on your link you will get paid for those clicks.
- You can login daily to see how many clicks you have got as well as how much money you have earned.

Paid to click ads and read ads

The sites that pay you to see ads or read them come under this category... There are a lot of sites available online some of them are listed below.

1. ClixSense

ClixSense is the most genuine PTC site & a lot of people are earning more than Rs.50, 000 from ClixSense in just a year time.

It's really very simple to join & work on ClixSense. These are the steps to sign up on ClixSense-

- Just visit the website & fill the signup form.
- After signup, you will receive validation link in your email. Click the link to validate your account.
- Then login to your ClixSense account with your username and password & complete the remaining other details of your profile.
- You are going to need to have a PayPal account.
- PayPal.com is free to join where you can add your bank account & receive money from PayPal to any of your bank account in India too. You receive the money from ClixSense through PayPal. ClixSense sends the money in your PayPal account & PayPal sends the money to your bank account.

2. NeoBux

This is also one of the best PTC sites. You can follow the similar procedure mentioned above to sign up and get started. I have seen many Neobux members making $3000 per month. So, it means that if you work hard or follow some steps then you can earn a real good income from it.

Remember – The most important point about PTC sites is that there are thousands of PTC sites present on the net but most of them are actually fake. Only a few of those sites are really trust-worthy & making payment to their members. But ClixSense & NeoBux are 2 sites which are powerful as well as trust-worthy and paying their members without fails.

Useful ways to Increase earning in PTC sites

It is not possible to increase your earning by spending more time on PTC sites because the ads are limited and there is no way to view more number of ads at a time than what the sites are providing.

The best solid ways to multiply your income from PTC sites

1. View all the ads daily. Make it a habit to view the ads everyday at a fixed time.
2. Refer the sites to your friends, relatives & other known people in your group. You will earn part of the income from each & every referral & multiply your income very high.
3. You can also opt to take their premium membership. Through this way, you will receive double commission for viewing the ads and also you will receive double commission when your referrals view the ads.

So this way you can earn regular money from PTC sites.

Get paid to take surveys

If you are looking for ways to make money online and if you can spend 1-2 hours daily then online surveys are the best way to earn nearly 10K to 20K per month.

Many national as well as international companies want to grow their business by increasing the sale of their products. They can do this if they know what people from each and every corner of the world, think about their products, their opinions about why they buy and don't buy a product.

By taking the feedback from the people, they can create a new product or improve the existing products according to their requirements.

Why somebody will spend its precious time in all these as giving the feedback and filling this online survey form takes time, people do not respond to such surveys when they don't get anything in return.

So, just because of this reason, these companies attract more and more people by giving some returns in terms of cash or shopping vouchers of popular online shopping sites or both so that they can spend at least 10-15 minutes for completing a survey job.

You can earn nearly Rs.20 to Rs.100 for filling 1 survey (in Indian currency). It mostly depends on the time it takes to complete a survey. Most of the companies send your income in your PayPal account.

So through this way you can earn money from online survey jobs. Some of the companies which provides online surveys to earn money or shopping vouchers from home are as follows -

1. Star Panel
2. iPanel Online India
3. Survey Head
4. Toluna India
5. Panel Place
6. Permission Research
7. Planet Pulse
8. Spider Metrix

9. Valued Opinions India
10. The Panel Station
11. https://earnably.com/

Pay per Action or sign ups

These companies pay you if someone just signs up with your link to their sites. They don't have to pay anything to signing up for these sites but still you will get paid for it. There are so many companies present in the market but I am familiar with these two, as these two also offer some other ways to earn extra income. They are-

1. **SFI** – It is a very old company. It provides a lot of ways to earn money referring people is one of them. They pay a real good income to refer people.
2. **Cash Carte** – It is also free to join and will pay you a good amount if someone signs up with your link.

Pay per downloads

Champcash – It is one of the best apps that pay you when someone downloads the app and signs up using your link. You will also earn some amount when someone signs up with your referrals link…

All these sites will also pay you money when your referrals earn something from these sites. It is a way through which you can earn a passive income. It can be a little slow way of earning money but instead of wasting your free time you can spend it in earning some extra income.

Earn money to sell photos

It was really shocking for me when I came to know that you can earn a real good monthly income just by selling some of your good photos online... It is a very common thing that we all go out of vacations and as everybody do, we click a lot of photos. Sometimes we click some pictures that are utterly beautiful like a very nice scenery, natural look of flower, birds, mountains, river, roads, or anything. Any of those pictures will be fine to earn money from this way.

This can be a source of passive income for you all. As you have to upload photos one time and each time when someone buys it you will earn money for it. As simple as that, right...

All the sites names that are listed below are the most popular ones in this field... You just have to sign up for them upload some photos to get approval from their side to start selling. Once they approve your uploaded photos then you can start uploading as much as images you want and earn a real good income from this way.

Some basic features to get approval of your photos is that your images should be in good quality plus clear and you can visit these sites to get a genuine idea about everything. Some of my friends are photographers and so they are earning nearly 100 thousand dollars monthly.

Don't think that if you are not a photographer then you cannot earn any money through this method. It is not like that anyone can upload good photos and earn money from them. If you don't have any photos to upload then you can take your smart phone and go out to get some beautiful clicks, that's it. And upload them to get approval and start earning…

Shutterstock is one of the best ones in this field, as it is a very much popular photos selling websites all around the web. Its popularity increases the chances of getting good sales from your photos. Fotolia is also good one... Getty images is also a popular one to start earning money from your photos... Each one pays you according to their payment plan from 10% to 60% per sale.

Below are the top 10 names that allow you to upload your good photos and earn money through each sale…for free of cost…

1. Shutterstock
2. istock

Get paid to listen music

Can you believe this that you can earn money even for listening songs or music online? But shock yourselves it is absolutely true as there is a place I know that is going to pay you for listening songs. You can sign up to this site for free and then start listening to the songs or music that is available or search for them to listen.

3 step procedure-

- Sign up
- Listen
- Earn.

Music Xray - https://www.musicxray.com/

We often spend our free time in listening to songs that we like or explore or find new music to get rid of boredom. Now just imagine you can get paid to do all this... It is a very good way to earn a good time-pass income while doing your daily routine. And if you are a music lover then it is a very good way of monthly income for you.

https://talent.welocalize.com/

You can also check this one, they hire freelances to listen to songs and convert them into text. A few more that will help you earning with music.

- https://current.us/
- https://radioearn.com/
- https://www.hitpredictor.com/
- https://cash4minutes.com/
- https://playlistpush.com/

Get paid to write Whatsapp status

Mostly everyone uses whatsapp nowadays. We all have used it so we knew already about what a 'whatsapp status' is. Some of us put different – different status daily or even many times a day.

But just think if you are getting paid for that then, you heard right there is a site I know which pays you to write various whatsapp statuses. They have a huge number of categories in which you can write good status and submit them.

You can sign up for this site for free and then first write 2 statuses in any category in the starting and submit them for first approval. When they approve your first 2 status then you can submit as much as statuses you want daily and earn a good monthly income from that.

Whatsstatus - https://www.whatsstatus.com/

Get paid to read jokes

I found this one accidently while searching for some other things. But it is absolutely true that you can get paid to read jokes….

Right to read jokes…...you will be getting paid…..

I am not kidding. This site also offers some other ways to earn money like earn to take surveys, earn to write articles, shop anything online etc…

But the best and easy one that I know is that when you sign up of this site and verified your e-mail address, then they send you jokes in your inbox nearly daily. You just have to follow the link given in the mail and read the joke, once you complete reading then you will be credited with the amount, as simple as that.

So, just sign up and start getting jokes in mail…to earn money or mobile recharge or shopping vouchers.

Below I have mentioned the name as well as the site that allows you to earn through this way.

Amulyam - http://www.amulyam.in/

Get paid to share a file

Everybody creates a lot of files, PDFs etc... You can also get paid to upload such files and when someone downloads it for free then you will earn a dollar for each download. It is free to join.

So, you just have to sign up of this site and upload files. After that you can share it to social networks to built audience and get more and more downloads. Use some catchy title so that people can't stop themselves to see what is present in you file.

Most important tip – Never try to click or download your own link or file as it will make the site think that you are trying to hack it or doing fraud with the help of them to earn a lot of money from them.

It is a real good way to earn money also can become a passive source of income with time. So, always keep this in mind to play safe and earn without any problem.

Share Cash - *https://sharecash.org/*

Get paid to write reviews

We love to explore things and talk about them. People are God gifted with the quality of giving their reviews on anything around them. And now you can earn money by writing honest reviews on products, movies, online sites, anything which you want to share their good or bad with world. This site is offering a good amount per honest review you post and share it with your friends on face book.

Now the question arises what to do and how to do. Well it's very simple to apply.

- Open Mouthshut.com and sign up for free.

- Put your profile picture (a mandatory step).

- Search the Product or Service, whose review you want to share with world. If the product or Service is not available in search section then just go and write a mouthpad. Where you can write about a new product.(It will take some time to check the mouthshut team to check your new mouthpad request and approve it)

- After writing the review. Share it on face book. Your job is completed.

- Now the team will approve your review. It can take some time to do so.

Remember

- You should upload your genuine profile picture.

- Use genuine Face book Profile of yours.

- You must share only one time as sharing multiple times won't help.

MOST IMPORTANT- The reviews should be honest and *not* copied from any other site. Words used in reviews should not be abusive or offensive.

Share it with your friends. As they can also share their reviews with the world and get rewarded.

Sell notes online to earn money

There are students who do not have the time or skills to create their set of notes and the only way out there for them is to outsource them. If you are good and precise in making notes, you can share your academic guides with the students who are ready to buy it through the internet.

Whether you believe it or not, there is a huge demand for your study material these days in the market and you can actually make a decent amount by selling notes online! Trust me…

According to me, there is no harm in sharing your notes to the needy for money. And besides, web technology has been improved a lot and so because of this keeping the old records for sale is much easier than ever before.

You may require mentioning your name, class, subject, etc. for selling your notes online. You can upload either your handwritten notes or digitally typed notes to the appropriate category according to it.

Earning a good income would depend on the demand for your subject you have chosen and how much your notes have been liked or found helpful.

There are some websites that are specifically meant for the people to sell notes. These sites are not in any specific order. Each website has its unique set of features, and you can prefer the one which suits or appeals you the most.

1. Studysoup

StudySoup is one of the most promising notes selling websites launched on the web nearly in the year of 2014. The homepage is actually full of testimonials of students making over a thousand $ per month.

Getting started with StudySoup is easy. You simply need to create a free account, and you're ready to go. However, to start selling StudySoup, you need to be from a university mentioned in their list of schools.

2. OneClass

If you are a student from the United States, Canada, Australia and New Zealand then you can definitely start earning from OneClass. Its range seems to be more diverse than the StudySoup. There are a lot of universities covered around the United States and Canada.

Thus, if your school doesn't list at StudySoup, you don't have to lose hope! OneClass boasts of millions of notes by around 800,000 university students. Besides, there's a question-answer section as well.

The interesting part of OneClass is that it pays you with gift cards from places such as Amazon, Starbucks and more. It might seem a great deal if you wanted to use your money that way, but it's a grave disadvantage if you need straightaway cash from your work.

3. Oxbridge Notes

Oxbridge Notes is yet another very good portal as well as popular with a buyer base of a large number of people. Also, it can be partner if you are from any of the below mentioned six countries-

- Australia,
- Ireland,
- Canada,
- New Zealand,
- United Kingdom and but obviously
- The United States.

If you got good notes, you can upload here and receive cash on a monthly basis. They will not reveal your name to the buyers, and you may leave from the site whenever you want. They need Notes, Essay Plans, Mind Maps, and Typed-up Notes from the outstanding students who got good grades in their academics.

However, you can't just register for a free account and get started directly. It is a little different the others. You need to fill a form, and if they like your details, they will invite you to join as a note seller.

4. Notesgen

Notesgen is an actually an online educational marketplace which was created nearly in the year of 2015. Now, I will come to a very special point that if you are an Indian, then you can really make use of this notes selling website..... You can earn a good income from your valuable tutorials.

Yes! Just upload your self-prepared academic notes in Notesgen, set price for others to purchase and get paid for every sale. Notesgen has a well-designed mobile app (both Android and iOS) to access the purchased content from anywhere, anytime.

The best part of Notesgen is that it doesn't let the buyers download the notes directly. Instead, it lets them view the notes in their mobile app or file viewer software.

5. Stuvia

If you really want to turn any of your notes or study material into cash, then it the exact place for you to achieve your goals! Stuvia accepts the study materials and summaries...... It can actually be an incredible marketplace to sell your notes online.....

It's very simple to use. Study guides from students are ordered here by ratings; the greater the ratings of your notes the greater are the changes of them appearing in a potential buyer's page... As simple as that....

You are going to be rewarded if people found your notes helpful or are happy with your work and vice versa..... To grab some really honest good ratings which will ultimately would lead to chunks of money, it recommends you to sell your notes initially for free....Don't worry about it as you can easily alter the price later on....

They also notify the potential buyers about the helpful study documents before their exams and thus you would get benefited by their active promotion.....

Below are some more sites that are quite popular for selling notes online...and earn some good income with it.

- NoteSale
- NoteUtopia
- StudentVIP
- Omega Notes
- Nexus Notes

You might be thinking that if you are not a student or you don't have any student in your house then you can't earn money through this way. But is not like you can upload your old notes or you ask your neighbors whether they have notes on any topic or not.

As you must remember that if you didn't have an idea about selling notes and earning money then they too will not have any idea about it. So, you can use their notes modify them a bit and then upload them to sell and earn.

Get paid to hear and write

Transcription is a form of data entry. In its basic form, transcription is typing directly from dictation or an audio file, though there are different kinds of transcription such as general, legal, medical transcription etc. All you need is the ability to understand what is being said, and type it directly and accurately into the computer.

The dictation source file may be a lecture, a conference call, a podcast, or simply someone taking notes and wanting them transcribed. You really don't need special training or a college degree for this. You can work at your own speed direct from home at any time of the day or night. It is more of a flexible job.

You are usually paid by the length of the audio, so it clearly means that the faster you can type the more you will earn but you must make this sure that your typing is absolutely accurate.

You can earn anywhere from $10 to $25 per hour you work, depending on the kind of transcription you're doing and the company you work for. There are some legitimate and trusted companies that actually hire people to work from home as transcribers.

If you're interested in earning money as a transcriptionist, you can have a look on these sites to get an idea about everything.

I have not given any detailed description but a general overview of these companies. You can personally visit them to get full knowledge about all the procedure....

1. Tigerfish

Tigerfish is one of the bigger companies in this field which is known for its work at home positions. The company has been around since 1989. It offers many different types of transcription work, including law enforcement, focus groups, and interviews.

2. SpeakWrite

SpeakWrite is an online transcription company that hires transcribers in the U.S. and Canada as independent contractors to work from home. According to the company, they serve over 65,000 legal, government, law enforcement, and other private sector clients. Their top contractors earn up to $3000 per month while the minimum earners make around $300 per month.

3. Transcribe Me

TranscribeMe is a good place to start as a beginner, as they do not require experience. Their pay rate is about $20 per audio hour. That's $.33 per audio minute. You must have a PayPal account as you get paid via PayPal.

4. Birch Creek Communications

Birch Creek is a good company to work for, as it allows beginners to work on projects that other companies may require selected experience for. They do a lot of corporate and legal transcription jobs, doing audio files for Social Security, Veterans Affairs, Immigration, as well as legal and corporate client's transcription. The pay depends on the type of project that you do for them.

5. 3Play Media

As an independent contractor, you decide which projects you want to work on, how much you want to work and when and where you want to work. You have to undergo a series of proficiency tests, need to be able to type at 75 words per minute, and also have to be able to do Internet research. In return, you should be able to earn between $10 and $30 per hour depending on the project and your efficiency.

6. AccuTran Global

Native English speakers looking for part-time work can try AccuTran Global. They pay out through PayPal or by check.

7. Transcriptions 'N' Translations

You may be interested in working for Transcriptions 'N' Translations, which operates out of Miami. They tend to have big projects with companies like the Discovery Channel and Animal Planet.

8. Casting Words

They hire freelance workers in from pretty much most countries. They actually have an extensive list of countries they accept workers from on their FAQ page.

Pay rate varies according to the quality of the recording, from $.60 per audio minute for a good recording up to $1.20 if the audio is poor quality. They pay via PayPal.

Below is some more websites that offers such jobs ...

- Alice Darling Audio Transcription Services
- GMR Transcription
- 1-888-TYPE-IT-UP
- Appenscribe
- Crowdsurf
- American High-Tech Transcription and Reporting
- Daily Transcription
- Terescription
- Neal R. Gross
- RNK Transcription

Get paid to read emails

You may think that it is not actually possible as you may have heard about some fraud websites. It may sound impossible but genuinely paying email reading jobs are there on the internet and well suited to people who are looking to make significant and steady income every day.

No matter which email service you use, you have the specific experience or not, you don't need any special skills to make money through this method. It is one of the easiest jobs by which you can easily make around $100-250 per month without making much effort.

There are various websites available where you can make some good extra money through this email reading jobs. However, you need to be extra careful as there are many scam websites available online.

But according to a good research here are some of the genuine websites that you can refer to **earn money online by reading emails**.

1. Matrixmails.com

Matrixmails.com is a brilliant website for generating money by reading emails since 2002. It is a free platform with *Google Page Rank 4* with absolutely no spam risk. All emails are sent to in-server email addresses supplied by them. They also offer both incentive and non-incentive based advertising solution at affordable prices. The following are the ways through which you will get paid.

- You get paid to read paid emails.
- You get paid to sign up offers with other applied terms.
- You also get paid to click and visit the sites.
- You can play games and writing articles for getting paid.
- You get paid to surf the internet and also for referring other people up to 6 levels.

Matrixmails also gives you an opportunity to earn lifetime bonuses, enabling you to get instant payment as well. The instant payment system is made via *AlertPay* with only $2 payout limit. You can easily **earn $25-$50 per hour** with your efforts.

2. Paisalive.com

If you want to make fast money without investing a single penny then *Paisalive.com* is the best platform to *earn money for reading emails*. It is one of the most convenient platforms for making money by reading emails that pays amount up to Rs.5 for reading mails in your inbox.

Now how to make money with it…You can follow the below steps…

- You can get Rs. 99 instantly just for signing up here in Paisalive.com
- If you refer 10 people, you get Rs. 10 immediately.
- After 10 referrals, you get Rs. 2 for each friend you refer.
- You can get Rs 0.25 to Rs. 5.00 by reading emails in your Paisalive inbox.
- You get Rs. 0.30 login incentive to Paisalive account in every 24 hours.

Paisalive.com pays the amount to the members once in 15 days, and the mode of payment is Cheque. The minimum amount required for payment request is Rs. 5oo.

3. Cash4offers.com

Cash4offers.com is another good website for generating extra revenue by working on a computer. It gives several ways to be rewarded your online activity. Once you become a Gold member, then you shall receive payment within 72 hours. All you need to do is read emails, take surveys, complete cash offers and trial, play online games, refer friends. You also get *$5.00 sign up bonus for just joining* the site.

4. Sendearings.com

Sendearnings.com is another good website from where you can make quick money online. The website adheres to strict guidelines of reading emails and getting paid.

Website works in 3 simple steps–

- **Sign up Process:** where you have to create your free account by clicking **JOIN NOW** button.

- **Activate Account:** You have to click the confirmation link to complete your registration by your email.

- **Earn Independently:** Earn unlimited cash by reading emails, take surveys, shop online, redeem coupons and more.

It pays you $1.00 for every email you read. If a member doesn't visit the site after signing up for at least once in six months, then his/her account gets deleted. You need a *minimum of $30 in your account* before you can request payment.

5. Moneymail.in

If you want to earn extra income then ***Moneymail.in*** is the right place for you. You can easily earn Rs. 10,000 per month by *just spending 15 minutes* daily. The concept of Moneymail is extremely simple which lets you earn money by reading emails online.

You can easily **earn Rs. 0.20 to 200 for every email** you read on the site ranked 1 on *Google Page*. In order to earn money, all you need to do is login daily in your account and read inbox emails. In other ways, it also works as a referring system by letting you earn around Rs. 100 for each member you add. So register now and start utilizing benefits of its services.

Get paid to tweet

You heard it right that you can get paid to write tweets and post them from your Tweeter Account. It needs to have a certain amount of followers but still there are a lot of ways available to get genuine followers.

1. Magpie
Magpie is the number one choice for marketers who seek to engage their target clientele in a conversation about their brand, business or products, providing an easy-to-use tool for viral marketing seeding with measurable results.

They believe that they help their clients to shift from last century's online advertising techniques to engaging people in a meaningful, interesting and transparent way in social networks and micro-blogging.

According to Mapie, if you have 1000 followers, you are capable of earning 200 USD per month. PayPal Minimum Payout is 50$.

2. TwitPub
TwitPub is just another fantastic way to monetize Twitter. The best way to be rewarded for generating quality content (or tweets) is to get paid for it. All you need to do is to have a Twitter account and set it to private (or protect your updates so it's not publicly visible) in your Twitter settings.

They pay through PayPal and Cheque. There Minimum Payout is 25$ (PayPal) and 50$ (Cheque)

3. RevTwt
Become a Revtwt publisher so you can earn money from your Twitter tweets, Face book status updates and wall posts! It is free to join. This may not work for everyone. To make money, you will need lots of real human followers who are the intended target audience of the ads.

Give it a try for a couple of days. It is free. If it works for you, stick around and make more money. If not, you are free to delete your account at any time. The Payout Options are PayPal and Cheque.

There Minimum Payout is 20$ (PayPal) and 100$ (Cheque)

4. Sponsored Tweets

Sponsored Tweets is a platform that helps you monetize Tweets created via Twitter. Just remember, this is a marketplace and you are competing with others for advertiser dollars. Set your price too high and you may scare advertisers away, too low and you may be short changing yourself.

5. TwtMob

Earn money every single time you tweet some of our cool content to your twitter followers including music videos, movie trailers, comedy jokes and more. Like I said…cool stuff! No get rich quick schemes and other BORING stuff that none care about.

Get paid to type captcha (captcha typing)

Captcha typing I am very much sure that you must have heard about his one… You type some characters mentioned in the box and get paid for typing them quickly… They nearly pay 1 $ for 1000 captchas you type…

It may seem that it is very low payment but as you increase your speed of typing them quickly and accurately you will be earning a lot more from this way… If you just spend 2-3 hours daily in this work then you can definitely earn as much as you want to earn from this method…

There are a huge number of sites are present around the web but the following are some very popular sites in this field… The best one is Megatypers….as per my knowledge and experience… But you sign up of that you are going to need an invitation code…

Don't worry about that you can easily find it on Google just search on Google for invitation code for sign up on Megatypers and then use any of the received codes from the search engine…. Protypers is also quite similar to Megatypers…

Here is a list of all those most popular ones in the field of captcha typing ---

1. Megatypers
2. 2captcha
3. Protypers
4. Kolotibablo
5. Captcha typers
6. Captcha 2 cash

Get paid by doing jobs from home

I have not mentioned it particularly that what kind of work you can do and earn from these sites as they provide a lot of opportunities to show your talent and earn according to that. You can enter as much as skills you have and then they will search for the jobs suitable according to your talent…. Once they have found they will recommend you and you can bid on them to get started and earn something from it…

You can see that Upwork is mentioned on the top of the list as the one big advantage of this sites that I personally know is that they are really good in the matter of making payments…

As per my knowledge they take the payment in advance from the job providers and then when you get your work approved they pay you. As the client had made the payment in the starting so they can't cheat you even after providing them with their work…after getting done completely..

You can show your skills with some tests results also… Upwork provide you with some free tests, you can take them any time and then let them appear with your profile to build an impression on the clients….

Below is the list of 10 nearly most popular sites who offer you to express your talent and earn a living from it….

1. Upwork.com
2. Freenlancer.com
3. Capitaltyping.com
4. Elance.com
5. Indeed.com
6. Fiverr.com
7. Elance-odesk.com
8. Monster.com
9. Clickworker.com
10. Axiondata.com

Publish e-books for free and earn royalty

If you are reading the e-version of this book then I am dame sure that you must be aware of this way of earning money online…

Yes… you got it right…. I am actually talking about KDP (Kindle Direct Publishing)…

It is an awesome platform from the great Amazon which allows you to publish your writings in the form of a book… specially an e-book… When I discovered this way of earning money online… I was quite mad with happiness, as the only thing I was good at or loved to do was nothing but writing….

There were a number of things present inside me that I always wanted to share with everybody out there. But in my own struggle of earning more and more money never allowed me to live in my world of writing….

When I found KDP I was so much excited that I decided to write books and publish them to earn money from it… It is really a blessing from Amazon as they don't take a single penny to publish your book in their huge market and even pays you for book sales…

Everything started on that day when I read a book on writing and publishing book on kindle… I was so much inspired by that book, that I wrote a book in the next 3 weeks itself… It was a huge confusion for me to select the topic about my book. But I thought that instead of finding new stories to write, it will be a lot better to first write about what I know already.

So, I wrote a book on 'how to earn 30k – 50k from home without investment' then 'how to start a business from home today' then 'Dear Dad' and then 'What went wrong – why he left me (11 common relationship mistakes done by her)' and still continuing writing books…. If you want you can visit my author page to get an idea of all the books…

You can see that the first 2 of my books are business books and the other 2 are relationship based… I am an online reseller myself so that is why I wrote about it in the first one… then the second book is about all those business ideas that I myself wanted to start or have seen people successfully earning from it… The third one that is based on the reality that happened between me and father and how I became alone in everything…..

The fourth one is specially based on the modern relationship mistakes done by woman and loses the only true love that they got in their lives… I wrote this one as I am aware of this fact that if this four letter word 'LOVE' is not present in our life then nothing can ever make sense in anybody's life….. I have seen this around me and really want to take a step to solve this problem and let everyone live happily with their true loves….

I have heard that you should write books only on one genre means if you wrote your first book about some business tip then you should continue writing books on that subject only… But I want to say this that if everybody does not has a doctorate on any particular subject then how he can continue writing on only one subject…

Everybody has their own experiences on various topics in their life. They all are unique in some way as what you experienced from particular situations in your own life can never be experienced by anybody else…

I have written what I learned from my own life… which is unique…and may be possible that it can prove to be helpful for you in your life…

Now, I will come straight to the point and explain you everything with some details. So, the procedure that I follow to write a book is that –

First decide what you want to write... To decide that start thinking as much as topics that comes in your mind when you think that you are going to write a book… Write all those topics on a paper.

Whenever you strike with a new topic write it down immediately on a paper to take a benefit from it someday. Now, from all those topics written by you is the first step towards your first book… Decide and finalize the topic on which you want to continue first and start writing a book to publish…

When you have decided the topic of your book then it is time to decide the table of contents… Follow the same procedure to write, first write the title of your book in the middle of a page and then write one by one that comes in your mind around it about that topic.... When you have written everything related to the title according to you then finalize the table of contents from this draft...

Now, you have an idea about the title of your book as well as the table of contents... This is the time to start filling your book with words...

You should be consistent as well as constant while writing your book. If you try to complete your book very very quickly then it is a huge possibility that you will get bored with it and will soon stop writing.

So, to prevent that you should write daily that means you should decide particular number of hours which you can invest daily to write your book... In this way you can complete your book as soon as possible without getting bored from it.

Always keep this in mind that 'getting your rough draft done is better than waiting to make it perfect'. It means that you should complete your rough draft of your book as soon as you can instead of trying to write a perfect book. Because you can make changes in your draft and convert it into a perfect book.

But if you will take a lot of time to finish your draft in the thought of making it a perfect book then it can take years to complete it. May be there is a huge possibility of you getting so bored with it that you will leave your book in middle and forget about it... I have seen and heard so many cases like this...

People think that writing a book is really very hard thing to do. But in reality if you follow some simple steps and procedure you can actually write a very good book in a very short period of time.

Now, your first draft is ready... you have to edit it. I know I have told you earlier that all the ways mentioned in this book are not going to cost you any money... So, I will guide you with what I did in the starting...

I actually had no money to invest in my career of writing as I was hardly earning anything to run my house. Then how could I have arranged money to invest in my new experiment. So, I tried to manage it on my own... I have worked under an editor for some time so I had an idea about some key points that an editor keeps in mind while editing anything.

- Read you book out loud at least 3 times...

- After that make all the changes that you think you should make in your book which you noticed while reading your book out loud.
- Now, read your book in front of anyone else. I will advise you to read it in front of a person who has a good habit of reading books or somebody who can give you an honest review about it. He can help you in further editing.
- Ask him about the lines that he found difficult to understand and which portion is quite boring to hear.
- Now, make changes according to his reviews...
- Editors try to make lines sounding a bit simple to read and understand by common people.
- So, edit your book according to it.
- Also they try to shorten sentences and increase the overall number of sentences or paragraphs, instead of writing big or long sentences...
- A book with very simple sentences to understand easily will be liked by a lot of people...especially common ones...
- So, follow these steps and edit your book...yourself....

Remember – When you start earning from your book then try to invest some money in editing, and marketing of the book to increase your overall book sales... I also did that…

You must have written the book in the word. Now just save your word file in html format and now you are ready to upload it to Kindle, it will format it in the form of an e-book on its own.

In the starting you can use Kindle's cover creator to design your e-book cover. It is free of cost to use... You can invest money in it after your start earning something from your book.

Upload everything, decide the price of your book and publish it… When it is 'live' on Amazon's worldwide sites then you can share its links to social networks and try to bring traffic to your book page and start getting sales from it.

Also join communities, create author's page on Amazon's author central page.

There is a lot more to do to get more and more profit from this way of earning... I will write one more book soon on this topic mentioning my own ways of success with Kindle...

This was the basic over view on publishing your book on Kindle without any investment and earning a good income from it...the detailed description of this topic will be mentioned in my upcoming book...

Sell public domain books

This is the special way for all those who have never ever written anything and never ever can write anything themselves… Also you don't have enough money to hire anybody and pay them to write it down for you… So, to make it easy for you to publish a book without actually even writing it is to upload already written books…..with public domain…

You can very easily get a good public domain book on the following places –

- Feedbooks.com
- Gutenberg.org/
- Manybooks.net

You can select books from these sites and download it to make some changes…like adding some pictures related to the book, author's biography or converting it into some other language…etc… or anything unique with those already written books. You can then upload it with a new cover designs and earn good money from its sales…

Design your own products and earn money

You might be thinking that if you have not done any course in designing then how you can earn money through this method. But don't worry about it as it is so easy to do that anyone can earn a good monthly income just by applying some simple efforts….

"MY DREAM STORE"

To start earn from this method just search "My Dream Store" on Google and you will find www.mydreamstore.in/ . Visit it and sign up using any of your social networks. This is the place where you can design your products, launch it then promote it to get orders.

This company manufactures the products designed by you and then delivers it directly to the customers when gets ordered by anybody. You can design t-shirts, phone covers and many more other things.

You don't have to add your profit in the prices as they will give you a share in each sale, you just have to design them, launch them and promote them. In this way you don't have to find wholesalers and crosscheck them as you can sell your own designed products.

Each and every detail is up to you as it is you who will decide how many pieces of your designed products are going to be manufactured and for how many days your products can be seen on the website to buy.

As it is really very easy to design and launch products on My Dream Store but still if you don't have any idea of designing and want full guidance about it then you can see videos on You-tube about designing products on my dream store. As You-tube is a very good place to learn new things as I invented this whole concept of My Dream Store on you-tube itself that too accidently while watching some other videos.

Remember one thing that it is not a mobile based website so you need a computer/laptop to design and launch products and then promote them. Don't worry if you don't have one of your own, you can go to cyber once in a week, design enough products for 1 week, launch them and promote them first on FB.

After that you can promote them everywhere else through your phone during the rest of the week. In this way you just have to spend 1 -2 hours in a week at cyber in designing and launching of your products and then can do the promotion of your products from home, whole week.

If you an artist, you can check this one - https://www.redbubble.com/about/selling

It is quite popular for personally designed merchandizes.

Upload videos and earn passive income

This is one of the most famous ways to earn money from online… You can upload videos, create your own You-tube channel and earn a good regular as well as passive income from it.…

It follows the same path as the blogging… Same as that procedure you have to find a particular topic, genre or concept on which you can make effective and informative videos about.

Then start making videos and upload them on the site… As like a blog post here also to get more and more traffic on your channel you have to share it on as much as places you can specially social networking sites…

Unlike a blog it is also not a way of earning money on the spot but if you continue doing it regularly with new and interesting videos. Then you can definitely make your You-Tube channel as a passive earning machine itself.…

Earn as an online tutor

If you can teach anything then it can become your way of earning money online…

There are a lot of sites available around the web who offers you this opportunity to earn from your own talent of teaching… Some sites also provide you permission to upload your own course and earn money from its sales…

Some of the free as well as famous places where you can earn through this way are as follows-

- Udemy.com
- italki
- SameSpeak

I have mentioned 3 sites above as they are totally different from each other...

Udemy is the place where you can upload or teach on various subjects... italki is the place where you can teach any language that you know perfectly or have a very good knowledge of it… You can teach English on SameSpeak...

As there are a large number of places around the world where people didn't know how to speak English perfectly... If you are really good in English or at least can speak clearly in English then you can definitely visit this one to get full knowledge of it about its joining procedure and other formalities….

Sell domains

This is not a forever method to earn money online but still you can earn a good amount from it. Suppose you have a blog or website or anybody you know want to sell the domain of their sites. Then you can promote it and try to sell it and earn something from it. You might be thinking that why would somebody want to buy someone else's site…

See it is like this that suppose you have a blog with lots and lots of daily traffic coming on it… But now you are unable to maintain that blog because of some personal reasons or simply want to start a different blog on some other topic... Or just you have so many blogs or websites and now you want to concentrate on only one.

It means that you will be unable to maintain posts on other blogs….then what to do with them. So, here is an easy solution for this problem you can put your domain on sale and earn a real profit from it…

I heard about a lady who had a food blog for 4 years but then suddenly she got married. Then she wanted to concentrate only on her personal life so she sold her domain. You will not believe that she got nearly 6000 $ for her domain…. So, this proves that you can actually earn from this method.

This was the way without investment but if you want to invest something then you can buy a domain first try to bring some good amount of traffic on that domain and then sale to make a good profit from it….

Earn from MLM scheme or direct selling companies

It is not the way that everybody refers you to but if it is free to apply then why can't we give it a try…. If you didn't earn anything then you lost nothing as you never invested anything. But think it like this that if you actually started earning a good regular income from this way then what….

No investment still got good returns… Some good direct selling companies that I can trust in India are Amway, Tupperware, Avon, Oriflame etc…. As they are reputed as well as trustworthy, they are paying their members regularly without any issues…frauds or melodrama…

Some of the common benefits that you can take from these companies are listed below-

- You will get a wide variety of good quality products to share, sell and earn profit.
- Each company will help you in growing your contacts as well as improving your status of living.
- Direct selling companies have certain levels and if you achieve those levels through your sales then you will get extra incentives, gifts, benefits, discounts etc… from the company too.
- After attaining a certain level in these companies they offer you free foreign tours, which not only just cover all your expenses but also give you money for shopping over there.
- It is a business of team-work, where if someone wants to join like you did and work for the company then you can help them in it and it will increase your earnings as well.
- One more extra benefit of these companies is that all of them are foreign based and offers imported products. And you know that imported products are always in trend.

Sell properties online – Be an online property broker

It is a very profitable offline work that you can also do online and expand it to increase your earnings… To earn a good income from this method follow the below steps-

- First find good properties which are for sale in your city or area...
- Grab some good pictures of it from nearly every angle…
- Also get complete knowledge about that property before putting it on sale...
- Once you got all these then you can upload it on your social networks and wait for inquiries...
- You can upload it on sites like quikr.com, 99acres.com, etc… to get more and more exposure…
- You can also make a FB page if you want to continue doing it and earn a regular income from it…
- This is also a kind of online reselling, the only difference here is that you are not selling clothes, jewellery, shoes or any other thing. In place of these things you are selling properties, something bigger and profitable…than the others...

Work from home – Amazon

Amazon has launched its Virtual Customer Service (VCS). It allows you to have a classic 9-5 job without the need of leaving the cozy home environment.

Rekindle program is yet another blessing from Amazon...

Amazon has launched a program named 'Rekindle', especially for women. It is providing a special opportunity to start all over again… Rekindle is an initiative from Amazon's side to provide a launch pad to women who have taken a break in their careers due to any of the circumstances... The company is trying to provide opportunities and support women to professionally re-integrate themselves once again and resume their career back…

According to them they have noticed that after taking any kind of breaks in their career women really want to resume their careers back. But due to lack of confidence and feeling of losing their skills once they used to have stops those to take any step forward…

So, the best part of this program is that Amazon rekindle really wants to provide a comfortable as well as flexible work environment that supports them and helps them completely to restart and re-continue their professional journey…

Now if you are also one of those who lost their careers in fulfilling some of your family responsibilities then Rekindle is the program especially designed for you from that 'angel' named 'Amazon'… Visit it to grab knowledge about all the available jobs and then if you find any particular one suitable for you then you should apply for it… Simple…

Find your desired job in Amazon through this link - https://amazon.jobs/en/

You can create a seller's account with Amazon then sell and earn commission. I know it doesn't sound easy but there's no harm in exploring, as you can trust Amazon.

Seller Central - https://sellercentral.amazon.in/

BONUS WAY !!

Get paid to answer questions –

- https://era.justanswer.com/#body
- https://www.maven.co/consultant#join
- https://www.experts123.com/
- https://www.6ya.com/experts

Conclusion

Now, you are aware of nearly most of the ways through which you can earn a good monthly or passive or both types of incomes online….

You can take the benefit of my online research of the last 6 years…. I have tried myself some of the ways and seen others earning from the other ways… So, I have mentioned it here in the book… A lot of people were not at all aware about all the ways through which they can actually earn and run their houses…

If you are also like me and really didn't want to work under somebody to earn for your family then select any one way from any of these and start applying your own efforts to be successful….

Just remember that anyone can only guide you but it is you who have to do the real work. No one is going to work in place of you, it is you who can decide your earnings according to your own efforts in it….

You have to apply effective efforts to start earning a good monthly income from any of these methods mentioned in this book and continue doing it to make a regular income….. Not only methods mentioned in this book but anything that you do in your life.

If you continue doing what you are doing then you have to believe in what you do…. The only key to success in any of your work is to believe in your work as well as the efforts you are applying….for it….

If you will not do this and think that it is not going to work then you can never be successful in any method….. To be successful in life follow this one step and keep on doing as well as believing in anything you do or want to do in future.

Never ever listen to the words of the crowd. They are common because they are listening to the world and so, do nothing unique to be in a list of 'out of the blues'. Don't be like them and face struggle your whole life….

Try these key aspects of life

- *Stop blaming everyone for your situations. Take responsibility of your life in your hands.*
- *You get whatever you decide for yourself, so think, think deeply 'what is it that you want for yourself'. Imagine the life, you would like to live.*
- *Stop over thinking without even trying. Be courageous and make decisions.*
- *Stop listening to what people say or are going to say or will say about you or your work.*
- *Think about 'what you want' 'why you want it' and 'how you can get it'. Then 'Decide your path'.*
- *Believe in YOURSELF. If you think you can do it. You WILL do it. I repeat – Only if you believe you can do it, you will do it.*
- *Just planning and believing is not enough. Take ACTION.*
- *Outcomes only depend on you so apply full efforts and*
- *Then continue doing it until you become successful.....*
- *Enjoy your life with your success....*

Follow this simple scheme to achieve your dream goals and be
SUCCESSFUL IN EVERY ASPECT OF YOUR LIFE!!!!!!

Thank you so much for purchasing this book and taking out your precious time to complete it. I hope this information helped you in some way or other. If it really did that please do share your experience or views through reviews. It would mean a lot. Thanks once again.

MAY YOU GET EVERYTHING YOU EVER DEEPLY DESIRE!
GOOD LUCK.

ADDITIONAL BONUS!!!

Nowadays there a lot of ways available to earn money from home through internet but if you don't know how to use a smart phone or computer or you aren't comfortable using gadgets then it is of no use for you. This is one of the biggest reasons why women are unable to start something. As they think that if they cannot use these gadgets then it is not at all possible for them to earn money from home or start a new business from home. If you are the ones who want to start a new business from your home but didn't have any good or efficient business ideas then don't worry at all. Here are **some simple local business ideas** that you can **start from your home** as soon as possible.

1. Prepare notes, assignments and projects
2. Baby sitting
3. Rent your clothes
4. Tiffin center
5. Coaching classes
6. Creative classes
7. Teach DIYs
8. Batter supply
9. Food stall – sell food from home
10. Home bakery
11. Supply homemade snacks
12. Organize "sale"
13. Mobile restaurant
14. Be a career counselor
15. Be a counselor or adviser
16. Design masks and sell them to shops or online.

HOW TO EARN 30K – 50K FROM HOME WITHOUT INVESTMENT

If you would like to read more about Online reselling, you can check this book from my author page – https://www.amazon.com/author/kapatil